Veterinary Service During the American Civil War

A Compilation

D1527093

Walter R. Heiss

PublishAmerica

Baltimore

First printing

ISBN: 1-4137-7326-5
PUBLISHED BY PUBLISHAMERICA, LLLP
www.publishamerica.com
Baltimore

Printed in the United States of America

Table of Contents

Acknowledgments

Dr. George E. Lewis, Jr. DVM, PHD, Colonel US Army (Retired) Jefferson, MD—Thanks to Dr. Lewis for sharing his knowledge and experience, which started me in the right direction and also for his critique of my work in progress and the final product.

Thanks to the following for their time and efforts in tracing, finding, and providing source documents and information to me through the facilities of their respective institutions:

Mary K. Mannix, MLS, MA, Manager, Maryland Room. C. Burr Artz, Central Library, Frederick, MD

Waneta Gagne, MLS, Librarian & Archivist, Maryland Room, C. Burr Artz, Central Library, Frederick, MD

Georgie Van Brocklin, Library Associate II, C. Burr Artz, Central Library, Frederick, MD

Steve L. Zerbe, Research Archivist, The Civil War Library and Museum, Philadelphia, PA

Jenifer Raisor, Curator of Collections, International Museum of the Horse, Kentucky Horse Park, Lexington, KY

C. Trenton Boyd, Director, Veterinary Medical Library, University of Missouri, Columbia, MO

Yolanda S. Heiss (16) for her "web searching," researching, typing, re-typing, copying, re-copying, composing, re-composing, editing and re-editing, all to keep a clean copy of this work before me at all times and still remain my *wife* after fifty-eight years.

Veterinary Service During the American Civil War

Introduction

Among all of the historical writings about the American Civil War, there is very limited coverage of veterinary service. The purpose of this document is to consolidate the findings of a selection of published research works and other writings. Each of these texts deals with veterinary service in the American military with emphasis on the Civil War period. This information, as assembled, is intended to chronicle the progress of that service with a brief look at its early history and a more detailed view through the years of the rebellion.

At the beginning of the Civil War, the United States had a horse population of approximately 7,500,000. Medical care providers for these animals were extremely limited in both numbers and capabilities. In fact, in 1861 there were only about fifty graduate veterinarians in the US, all of whom were schooled abroad and most were foreign born. Although three veterinary schools were established during the decade of the fifties, only one survived. The survivor was the New York College of Veterinary Surgeons founded in 1857. The first graduates were a class of two in 1867.

Despite the obvious dearth of what could be considered "real veterinarians" (a person skilled in treating the injuries or diseases of animals; a veterinary), this document uses no less than twenty combinations of terms for animal caregivers. There are only three of the twenty terms used that could be considered as defining a professional veterinarian. These are "degreed veterinarian," "graduate veterinarian," and "graduate veterinary surgeon as a commissioned officer." Those remaining range from "horse doctor" to "practitioners" to "farriers, as veterinary surgeons."

The extent to which the latter three named were qualified is a matter of conjecture. The same is true of the rest. Some could have earned their "titles" through necessity such as stock producers. Many had to be their own horse doctors. Farriers, in some instances, gained their veterinary status by practical experience. Others had some training plus experience, and some were simply charlatans. By whatever title and in whatever numbers, this is the cadre of animal caregivers with which the Union entered the Civil War. The Confederacy was no better off.

April 12, 1861, dawned and the country split apart. The two nations were each about to embark on programs of animal procurement, management, and medical care, the dimensions of which had never before been seen.

Hundreds of thousands of horses and mules were processed through the remount systems of both sides. The animals had to be tended to in one way or another. They had to be supplied with harnesses and saddles, and be shod, fed, and sheltered. Tens of thousands became sick or wounded and needed medical care. Thousands of these became disabled or perished and had to be replaced. The demands on quartermasters, impressment officers, "veterinarians" and farriers were staggering. The Union was able to cope with this enormous burden and won the war. The Confederacy could not cope and their cause was lost.[7]

The Union Side

A merican military veterinary medicine or care is almost as old as the American military itself. By a letter dated December 16, 1776, General George Washington directed the establishment of "farrier-veterinary" services in the horse artillery.[5,6]

The American cavalry was formed in 1777. On March 5, 1792, Congress created one squadron of light dragoons of four troops and authorized one farrier for each troop to shoe and treat horses.[1,5] The pay was $8 per month. In 1798, the number of farriers was increased from four to ten, and the pay was increased from $8 to $10 per month. From 1802 to 1808, neither the cavalry nor farriers were part of the army. Then, in 1808, Congress authorized a regiment of cavalry and provided for eight farriers.[4]

During the War of 1812, farriers were assigned to the horse artillery.[1,4] At the end of the war in 1814, however, farriers were dropped from military identification probably because of the reduced use of mounted combat units.[4,5] The term "farrier" as used in this writing applies, for the most part, to a combination horseshoer and horse doctor. Dating back to 1356, however, the term "farrier" was exclusive to veterinarians who had formed a British guild, "The Worshipful Company of Farriers." By the 19th century, though, the term was applied indiscriminately to horseshoers and horse doctors as if they were the same individuals, which in many instances they were.[3,4]

America began the trek toward the West, and in 1830 Congress passed the Removal Act, which displaced Native Americans living east of the Mississippi to points west. The ensuing territorial battles with the established native inhabitants and the relocated Indians created the need for military protection and enforcement.[1] To accomplish this, Congress in 1832 authorized the US Mounted Battalion with six companies of one hundred volunteers each. The volunteers furnished their own horses and equipment and were paid one dollar per day.[1]

In 1833, Congress approved a regular army unit, a regiment of blue-uniformed Dragoons with strength of 750 men in ten companies, A through J. By 1836, an Indian uprising by the Seminoles prompted Congress to establish a regiment of light-coated Dragoons to handle the Florida skirmishes. Farrier positions, which had been dropped from the military after the War of 1812, were reinstated to the regiments formed in 1833 and 1836.[1,4] There were ten farriers for each of the two regiments.[4]

The Army general regulations of 1834 and 1835 used the term "veterinary surgeon" for the first time and mentioned a Veterinary Department of Cavalry. The regulations discussed the qualifications and competence of the veterinary surgeon in fulfilling his duties, but since it isn't clear that there were actually veterinarians in the army at that time, and since it is equally unclear as to the nature of the station and rank of this position, it is assumed that the term may have referred to farriers.[1,4,5] If not farriers, another possibility is that any individual hired for the position was a civilian rather than a soldier. This is apparent from regimental reports for 1835, which reveal that regimental commanders were contracting with private veterinarians to tend and treat their horses and paying them from their units' "contingent funds."[3]

The 1849 Appropriations Act appears to be the first congressional authorization for hiring and paying veterinary surgeons. There is, however, speculation that the Quartermaster's Department was considering engaging civilian veterinarians as far back as 1837. The

Act of August 14, 1848 (Fiscal Year-1849), established this authority. It charged the Quartermaster's Department with the full responsibility for the hiring and paying. The funds were to be controlled and accounted for as "incidental expenses" in the department's annual report.[3,4,5] Regimental commanders now had some relief in not having to appropriate their regimental funds for medical services for their horses.

Veterinary service didn't progress much with the Mexican War (1846-1848). All horse doctors were farriers. In 1849, the year after the Mexican War ended, the army did employ a limited number of civilian veterinarians.[4] There was no evidence of any effort or suggestion to enlist horse doctors for full-time military service to be assigned to mounted units.

Keep in mind that at this time there were no veterinary colleges in the United States. Every degreed veterinarian was foreign trained while others were accredited by virtue of their experience.[3,5] Despite this, Army Regulations of 1835 charged the Inspector General to do performance evaluations of veterinary surgeons. The question of how the Inspector General would perform legitimate evaluations, lacking academically developed criteria against which to make such evaluation, remains to be answered.

There were those who saw the need for trained veterinarians for the military. In 1853, Quartermaster General Thomas S. Jesup urged Congress to establish an army veterinary corps and include a school as a source of instruction for mounted officers and candidates for the veterinary corps.[3,18]

Captain George B. McClellan, drawing on his observations of veterinary schools in France, Prussia, and Austria in 1855 and 1856, advised his superiors that "To the staff of each (mounted) regiment there should be added a chief veterinary with the rank of sergeant major or even as a commissioned officer." To provide for a source of practitioners: "A veterinary school should be attached to the (Cavalry School) for the instruction of officers and veterinaries." Neither Jesup's nor McClellan's urgings stimulated any action.[3]

In 1857, Colonel William J. Hardee, Commandant of Cadets at West Point, introduced a formal course in equitation with a segment of instruction on the "Veterinary Art." His text was from William Youatt's widely respected and detailed treatise on the horse. He used papier-mâché models as aides for lessons in equine anatomy.[3]

Although the government was dragging its feet on formalizing veterinary education, the decade of the 1850s did see the founding of several locally operated colleges. In 1852, The Veterinary College of Philadelphia was founded followed by the Boston Veterinary Institute in 1854. Both of these institutions failed without graduating any doctors.[5]

More successful were the efforts of Captain John C. Ralston. He was a graduate of London Veterinary College and served as a veterinarian in the British Army. Captain Ralston was involved in the organization of the New York College of Veterinary Surgeons in 1857 and became president of that institution. He goaded the United States in his essay, "The Veterinary Science and Art," intended for publication in the annual report on agriculture presented by the Commissioner of Patents in 1859.[3,5] Dr. Ralston stated in the report, "In this country, the veterinary science appears to have suffered, and is still allowed to suffer, unaccountably and most undeserved neglect, in an educational or duly qualified point of view."[5]

The essay included an overview of the development of veterinary medicine in Europe with the suggestion that advancements such as those were long overdue in the United States. He concluded by outlining the benefits that would result from the establishment of a veterinary corps within the U.S. Army.[3]

Shortly after the Civil War broke out, President Lincoln issued a presidential proclamation calling for the mobilization of military forces. Some Regular Army units were ordered into new positions, and the requested state militias, volunteers, and the recruitment of Navy seamen helped fill the ranks of needed personnel. Eleven new regiments, which included one of cavalry designated the 3rd Cavalry Regiment, increased the Regular Army.[2]

With this action, and right after the Union loss at the First Battle of Bull Run (First Manassas), Congress authorized mobilization of 500,000 volunteers on July 22, 1861, and then on July 25 authorized another 500,000 men.[1,2,5]

Congress confirmed the presidential proclamation that established the Regular Army 3rd Cavalry Regiment. The organization structure of this new regiment differed from that of the then-existing Regular mounted regiments. The new regiment was divided into three battalions and each battalion was subdivided into four companies, totaling twelve companies for the regiment.

The complement consisted of approximately 1,100 men, both officers and enlisted. The law authorized one veterinary sergeant for each of the three battalions, and each of the twelve regimental companies had one farrier.[1,2] It is assumed that the veterinary sergeant had the duty of supervising the farriers assigned to each of the regimental companies. His pay was set at $17 per month with the rank equivalent to a sergeant of cavalry, including allowances.[4,5] However, there was neither unique insignia nor other identification to distinguish the veterinary sergeant from any other sergeant of the line.[3]

The organizational structure of the 3rd Cavalry Regiment was at that time limited to that particular regiment. The five existing Regular mounted regiments at full strength would each have had about 660 officers and enlisted personnel. They each had ten companies and each company had one farrier.[2]

The structure of the U.S. Cavalry, as a whole, was in an extensive state of flux. Until the Act of July 29, 1861, when the 3rd Cavalry Regiment was formed, the cavalry service was composed of the 1st and 2nd Dragoon Regiments, the Mounted Riflemen Regiment, and the 1st and 2nd Cavalry Regiments.[2] The veterinary complements of each of these units were previously discussed.

On August 31, 1861, all of the existing cavalry units, by whatever name, were renamed as Cavalry Regiments 1st through 6th. By the Act of July 17, 1862, all six regiments were reorganized to assume the three-battalion, twelve-company format. The battalion veterinary sergeant was abolished and replaced by a chief farrier or blacksmith. The twelve company farriers remained.[2,3]

There is no known official reason for the elimination of the veterinary sergeant position. There are, however, some assumptions or opinions as to why. Since the rank really had no special recognition, some evidence suggests that where positions were filled, the persons occupying them were not qualified as either sergeants or veterinarians but were, in fact, farriers or blacksmiths.[2]

Although farriers were part of US mounted units since 1792, opinions of their abilities and accomplishments were in some instances less than impressive. One opinion, for example, states "According to the testimony of old soldiers…it fell to the lot of the shoeing-smith or farrier not only to adjust the shoes but to attend also to the sick and disabled [horses] and to superintend the administration of medicines. Usually the treatment was determined not so much by the nature of the complaint as by the drug that happened to be nearest at hand."[3]

John Stewart, an Edinburgh-educated veterinarian, assessed farriers in his writings "Stable Economy" as follows—"Horseshoers and village blacksmiths form another class…Being ignorant of anatomy and physiology, they never improve beyond a certain point. Most of them have a few books, of which the bad mislead them, and the good puzzle them. Give them a telescope view of the moon, and they instantly become astronomers. To such people is the world indebted for all kinds of quackery and a good deal of knavery."[3] So much for opinions of farriers.

As to the demise of the short-lived veterinary sergeant position, the rank lasted just one year. During that brief trial period, there were only three openings for veterinary sergeants in the entire army. There are many opinions as to why the veterinary sergeant rank vanished so quickly. One researcher, having inspected the Regiment of Cavalry Organization Chart for 1861, noted a significant increase in the number of "buck" sergeants, from 48 to 60. This increase of twelve raised each company allotment from four sergeants to five. There were no increases in other non-commissioned officers.[3]

This action may have permitted the cavalry to assign a "veterinary sergeant" to each company without identifying them as such. Legislation had removed the title, but it didn't remove the position. Also, since the position lacked distinguishing features in the way of insignia, pay or emoluments, a sergeant was simply a sergeant.[3]

A more specific argument about the elimination of the veterinary sergeant title was stated by Colonels Louis A. Merillat and Delwin M. Campbell in their *Veterinary Military History of the United States* (1935). Acknowledging that the 1861 establishment of the veterinary sergeant was a step toward a true Veterinary Corps, they went on to say— "[The position of veterinary sergeant] was not used to the best advantage. No effort appears to have been made at first to assign even non-graduate veterinary practitioners to these jobs, but instead to a very considerable extent, early in the war, the new grade with increased pay (over that of a private) was used as a reward for faithful old and frequently useless soldiers who were incapacitated for other duties, and in some instances for undesirable old soldiers who were not wanted elsewhere."[3,17]

Another historian of military veterinary medicine, A. A. Holcombe, reported "[The veterinary sergeant] positions were awarded, as a rule, to shoeing-smiths, farriers or peripatetic quacks who had imbibed empirical ideas of the most radical sort regarding the efficacy of certain remedial agents in the treatment of disease and of the value of their own very limited knowledge."[3,17]

There is additional speculation concerning the abolishment of the veterinary sergeant position, including one that Congress anticipated: the potential for (if not the actual existence of) cronyism and "good-old-boy-ism" and acted to remove the temptation. Whatever the reason, the veterinary sergeant position was gone, and the military was yet to have a veterinarian in uniform.[3]

Evidence indicates that Congress was indifferent toward the veterinary practitioners with little regard for their station, education, or qualifications. There is no evidence that Congress gave any consideration to engaging the fifty known graduate veterinarians in the country in 1861 to help form the beginnings of a competent veterinary service.[2,3]

The government's indifference to the army's veterinary needs is supported by the fact that during the entire fiscal year of 1861 (July 1, 1860 - June 30, 1861) only $168.50 was expended to hire civilian veterinarians.[3,4,5,18,20] During the remaining fiscal years of the war (July 1, 1861 thru June 30, 1865), only $93,666.47 was spent for "hire of veterinary surgeons."[1,2,4,5,18,20] Note this amount is for "hire of veterinary surgeons," which can be assumed were civilian practitioners hired and paid by the Quartermaster Department for the entire army. The names of these men are not known; neither are their places of employment nor their professional qualifications, if any.

Recorded on the same Quartermaster Department reports was $323,964.77 for "medicine for horses and mules."[2,3,20] Again the cost was incurred for the entire army. Interesting that for every dollar spent for a veterinary surgeon's services, $3.46 was spent for medicines. The "hired veterinary surgeons" must have been generous or liberal with their medical dosages. Perhaps a share of the medicines reported as purchased were prescribed or used by veterinary surgeons, farriers, or other practitioners within the ranks, whose pay was from their units or organizations' funds, but not clearly identified.

Although there isn't a direct connection, the War Department General Orders No. 195, May 12, 1864, and Adjutant General's Office Special Orders No. 137 providing for procurement of "horse medicines" and establishing a Standard Table for Horse Medicines and Supplies could well identify with the medicine cost reported by the Quartermaster.[2,17]

General Orders No. 195 provides: "The subjoined standard supply table of horse medicines, with regulations for the government of the Veterinary Department of the Army, prepared by a board of officers convened by Special Orders No. 137, current series, from this office, have been adopted and are published for the information and guidance of all concerned."[20]

This supply table, shown on the following page, set the standard of horse medicines for the army in field service and in hospital service. Allowances were identified in quantities for three months' use, in increments of 100, 200, 500 and 1,000 horses for each of the two services. The allowances were greater for use in the hospitals.[20]

Articles	Quantities for three months. For field service: 100 hoses	For field service: 200 horses	For field service: 500 horses	For field service: 1000 horses	For hospital service: 100 horses	For hospital service: 200 horses	For hospital service: 500 horses	For hospital service: 1000 horses
Aloes ... ounces....	1	2	3	4	2	4	6	8
Alcohol ... gallons....	¼	½	1	1¾	½	1	2	3½
Asafetida ... pounds....	¼	½	¾	1	½	1	1½	2
Alum ... do....	1	2	4	8	2	4	8	16
Blister liquid ... quarts....	½	1	2	3	1	2	4	6
Bluestone ... pounds....	½	¾	1	2	1	1½	2	4
Borax ... do....	1	1½	3	4	2	3	6	8
Calomel ... do....	⅛	¼	½	¾	¾	½	1	1½
Castile Soap ... do....	10	15	20	30	20	30	40	60
Grounds Flaxseed ... do....	8	10	15	20	16	20	30	40
Hartshorn ... gallons....	¼	½	¾	1	½	1	1½	2
Lunar caustic ... (ounces)....	¼	½	¾	1	½	1	1½	2
Laudanum ... quarts....	1	1½	2	4	2	3	4	8
Simple cerate ... pounds....	2½	5	5	10	5	10	10	20
Mercurial ointment ... do....	½	1	1½	2	1	2	3	4
Mustang liniment ... bottles....	2	3	4	6	4	6	8	12
Olive oil ... gallons....	½	1	2	3	1	2	4	6
Oil, linseed ... do....	½	1	2	3	1	2	4	6
Turpentine ... do....	¼	½	1	1¾	½	1	2	3½
Powell's liniment ... bottles....	2	3	4	6	4	6	8	12
Resin ... pounds....	½	1	1½	2	1	2	3	4
Salts ... do....	2	3	4	6	4	6	8	12
Sulphur ... do....	¼	½	1	2	½	1	2	4
Saltpeter ... do....	1	2	3	5	2	4	6	10
Sweet spirits niter ... quarts....	½	1	2	3	1	2	4	6
Sugar lead ... pounds....	1	2	4	5	2	4	8	10
Tar ... gallons....	¼	½	1	1¾	½	1	2	3½
Tartar emetic ... pounds....	¼	½	¾	1	½	1	1½	2
DRESSINGS								
Adhesive plaster ... yards....	1	1½	2	4	2	3	4	8
Muslin (coarse) ... do....	10	12	15	20	20	24	30	40
Red flannel (coarse) ... do....	2	3	4	6	4	6	8	12
Sponge ... pounds....	¾	1½	3	4	1½	3	6	8
Silk for ligature ... ounces....	¼	¼	½	1	½	½	1	2
INSTRUMENTS								
Abscess knife (2 blades) ...	1	1	1	1	2	2	2	2
Ball forceps ... Number...	1	1	1	1	2	2	2	2
Corkscrews ... do....	1	1	1	1	2	2	2	2
Funnels ... do....	1	1	1	1	2	2	2	2
Graduate glasses ... do....	1	1	1	1	2	2	2	2
Mortar and Pestles (iron) ... do....	1	1	1	1	2	2	2	2
Needles ... dozen...	½	½	½	½	1	1	1	1
Probes ... number...	1	1	1	1	2	2	2	2
Rowling needles ... do....	1	1	1	1	2	2	2	2
Scales and weights ... do....	1	1	1	1	2	2	2	2
Springs (syringes) ... do....	1	1	1	1	2	2	2	2
Spring lancet ... do....	1	1	1	1	2	2	2	2
Straight scissors ... do....	1	1	1	1	2	2	2	2
Spatulas ... do....	1	1	1	1	2	2	2	2
Trocar ... do....	1	1	1	1	2	2	2	2
Tenaculum ... do....	1	1	1	1	2	2	2	2

INTERNATIONAL MUSEUM OF THE HORSE

DOSES FOR THE HORSE.

Name of Drug.	Action and Use.	Dose.	Antidote.
Aloes.	Laxative and Tonic.	1-2 to 1 oz.	
Alum.	Astringent.	½ to 3 drs.	
Anise Seed.	Aromatic and Stomachic.	1-2 to 2 ozs.	
Aqua Ammonia.	Stimulant and Antacid.	1 to 4 drs.	Vinegar.
Arsenic.	Alterative and Tonic. Used for Paralysis, Mange, etc.	1 to 5 grs.	Magnesia and oil.
Assfœtida.	Anti-spasmodic, Coughs, etc.	1 to 3 drs.	
Bicarbonate of Potash.	Diuretic and Antacid. Good for Rheumatism.	3 to 5 drs.	Vinegar and raw Linseed Oil.
Bismuth.	For Chronic Diarrhœa, etc.	1-2 to 1 oz.	
Black Antimony.	Promotes the Secretions.	1-4 to 1-2 dr.	Infus'n of oak bark. Give also lins'd oil.
Blue Vitriol.	Astringent and Tonic.	1-2 to 1 dr.	Eggs, Milk, etc.
Calomel.	Cathartic.	10 to 40 grs.	Eggs and Milk.
Camphor.	Anti-spasmodic.	1-2 to 1 dr.	
Cantharides.	Diuretic and Stimulant.	3 to 6 grs.	
Carbolic Acid.	Externally and Disinfectant.		Eggs; soap; gruel.
Castor Oil.	Cathartic.	1 2 to 1 pt.	
Cayenne.	Stimulant and Carminative.	5 to 25 grs.	
Chlorate of Potash.	Diuretic. Given for Bloating, etc.	1-2 to 2 drs.	
Copperas.	Tonic and Astringent.	¼ to 1½ drs	
Croton Oil.	Powerful Purgative.	10 to 15 d'p's	Opium.
Digitalis leaf.	Sedative and Diuretic.	10 to 20 grs.	Stimulate.
Epsom Salts.	Cathartic and Febrifuge.	2 to 8 ozs.	
Ether.	Anti-spasmodic.	1-2 to 2 ozs.	
Fowler's Solution	Used for Skin diseases. See Arsenic, a preparation of.	1 to 4 drs.	Hydrated peroxide of Iron.
Gentian Root.	Tonic.	to 2 drs.	
Ginger.	Tonic, Stimulant and Stomachic. Used for Flatulent Colic, Dyspepsia, etc.	2 to 5 drs.	
Glauber's Salts.	Cathartic.	6 to 12 ozs.	
Iodide of Potassium.	Diuretic and Alterative. Used for Rheumatism, Dropsy, Enlarged Glands, etc.	1-2 to 1 1-2 drs.	Give freely starch or flour, with water largely.
Linseed Oil, Raw	Cathartic and Nutritive.	1 to 2 pts.	
Magnesia.	For colts as an Antacid and Laxative.	1-4 to 1 oz.	
Mercurial Ointment.	Used for Mange, Itch, Lice, and other parasites.		Whites of Eggs with milk given freely. Saleratus, followed quickly by copperas, both dissolved in water.
Nux Vomica.	Nervous stimulant. Used for Paralysis.	15 to 25 grs.	
Opium.	Anodyne and Anti-spasmodic. Given in Colic, Inflammation of Bowels, Diarrhœa, etc.	1-4 to 1 dr.	Belladonna, strong coffee, brandy and ammonia. Dash cold water on, and keep the horse moving.
Prepared Chalk.	Antacid.	1-2 to 1 oz.	
Quinine.	Tonic. Given during convalescence.	15 to 50 grs.	Linseed oil largely.
Saltpetre.	Diuretic and Febrifuge.	1 to 3 drs.	Raw.
Soda Bicarb.	Similar to Bicarb. Potash.	3 to 8 drs.	
Soda Sulphite.	Antiseptic and Alterative. Used for Blood diseases.	1-2 to 1 oz.	
Solution of Lime.	Antacid, used as an antidote to poisoning by acids.	4 to 6 ozs.	
Spirits of Chloroform.	Anodyne and Anti-spasmodic.	1 to 2 ozs.	
Strychnia.	Tonic and Stimulant. Used for Paralysis.	1-2 to 1 gr.	Tobacco.
Sulphur.	Alterative and Laxative. Used for Skin diseases and Rheumatism.	1-2 to 2 ozs.	
Sweet Spirits of Nitre.	Diuretic and Diaphoretic.	¼ to 1½ ozs	
Tannic Acid.	Astringent.	20 to 40 grs.	Tannic Acid.
Tartar Emetic.	Sedative and Alterative.	1-8 to 1-2 dr.	Give a small doses of Nux Vomica, and stimulants largely, and keep moving.
Tincture of Aconite Root.	Sedative. Used for lung fever, etc.	15 to 25 d'p's	
Tincture of Cantharides.	Stimulant and Tonic.	1 to 2 ozs.	
Tincture Ergot.	Parturient.	1 to 2 ozs.	
Tincture Iodine.	Used externally.		
Tincture Iron.	Tonic and Astringent. Used for Typhoid diseases.	1-2 to 1 oz.	
Tr. Nux Vomica.	Tonic. Stimulant in Paralysis and Dyspepsia.	2 to 4 drs.	See Nux Vomica.
Tincture Opium.	Anodyne and Anti-spasmodic.	1 to 2 ozs.	See Opium.
White Vitriol.	Astringent. Used for cuts, wounds and sores, in solution.	5 to 15 grs.	Milk, eggs and flour.

FROM "THE HORSE AND HIS DISEASES," BY DR. B. J. KENDALL, 1964

20

With these prescribed allowances, it's probable that the veterinarian was a pharmacist as well. Absent from the list were allowances for such instruments as thermometers and stethoscopes. There were few disinfectants.[2]

The order was not without substance. Proper use of medicines and dressings was insured by placing the responsibility for loss, damage, and the official use of these supplies with the veterinary surgeons. Except in "extreme emergencies" no deviation from the list was allowed. These orders were to remain unchanged for the next twelve years.[17,20]

Interestingly enough all of these veterinary services and supplies were procured, paid for, and distributed by the Quartermaster Department and reported by them as two line items in sums, with little or no definition.

If as is surmised, the details and allowances for the supplies were covered by War Department General Orders No. 195, it is possible or maybe even probable that the names of the veterinary surgeons and where they served were lost somewhere in the shuffle between the bureaucracies.

Finally on March 3, 1863, Congress authorized another reorganization of all six Cavalry Regiments. It introduced the word surgeons by creating one veterinary surgeon position for each regiment and two farriers or blacksmiths for each of the twelve companies. Note that the three-battalion structure was abandoned.[2] Up until this time in 1863, there were only six "contract veterinarians" in the U. S. Army.[5,6,17]

It is possible that someone involved in drafting this legislation recalled the recommendation made in 1857 by then Captain George B. McClellan that "To the staff of each mounted regiment there should be added a chief veterinary with the rank of sergeant major or even as a commissioned officer."

Was this act of Congress the impetus that would supply the veterinary expertise so sorely needed in the rapidly expanding cavalry? It could be assumed that this might be true. If a regiment was manned at full strength, the veterinary surgeon, probably operating out of regimental headquarters, had what might be considered a staff of twenty-four assistants, two farriers/blacksmiths for each of the twelve companies in the regiment.

The veterinary surgeon authorized by Sec. 37 of the Act of March 3, 1863, was an entirely new breed. Although he was not a commissioned officer (that wouldn't happen until 1916), he was appointed at the highest rank for a non-commissioned officer, that of sergeant major. Compensation was set by law at $75 per month, which was equivalent to a lieutenant's pay.[2,10]

Terms of the appointment of a veterinary surgeon implied, however, that he would not be regarded as an enlisted man. General Orders No. 259, 1863 provided the following:[2,3,10,17]

1.   He shall be nominated by a board of three regimental officers next in rank to the commanding officer.
2.   His name will then be transmitted to the Chief of the Cavalry Bureau.
3.   Chief of the Cavalry Bureau will submit his name to the Secretary of War for appointment.
4.   A record of his appointment will be kept in the Adjutant General's office.

The veterinary surgeon had all the privileges of an appointment. He could resign his appointment and his resignation would be acted upon as if he were an officer.[10]

Although the legislation was soft on the specifics of his duties and qualifications, they were stated to include:[10]

1.   Care and cure of sick and disabled horses.
2.   Considerable education involving knowledge of the anatomy and physiology of the horse.
3.   Knowledge of chemistry sufficient to understand the character and use of chemicals and medicines used to treat horses.
4.   A practical knowledge and experience in diseases to which horses are subject.

5.   Assigned responsibility for horse medicine and supplies used with accountability to the regimental quartermaster for the expenditures incurred for these items.

Nothing is mentioned in the records about what the veterinary surgeon's uniform should be and the law says nothing about an identifying insignia. It is assumed that despite his unique position, he would wear the uniform and chevrons of a sergeant major. In one incident, however, an insignia was reported to have been worn.

The furious Battle of Brandy Station, Virginia, June 9, 1863, pitted the cavalries of Confederate Major General "Jeb" Stuart and Union Major General A. A. Pleasonton against each other.[1,2,5,8] Many consider the battle a true cavalry battle in the Napoleonic tradition with pistols and sabers rather than carbines.[12] With approximately 19,000 saber-wielding troopers between the two sides, their mounts suffered an enormous number of saber slashes and bullet wounds. General Pleasonton's command was set up in a corps-division-brigade-regiment configuration. Imagine the confusion this organizational structure probably caused. The corps consisted of three divisions with two brigades each. The brigades each had four regiments with twelve companies each.[2]

Had the corps been manned to its authorized strength, which it probably wasn't, it would have had 24 regiments with 24 veterinary surgeons and 288 companies with 576 farriers. By sheer size the organization was not conducive to opening channels of communication between the regimental veterinary surgeons. As a consequence, there was no system for evacuation of wounded horses from the combat regiments. Through this all, there possibly were a few veterinary surgeons who established their identity by wearing horseshoe-shaped brassards on their sleeves.[2] (See Organization Chart.)

The discussion on identifying insignia ends with no mention as to what, if anything, was accomplished. Perhaps the lack of emphasis on an official prescribed insignia for the veterinary surgeon was due to the heretofore lack of interest in the position itself.

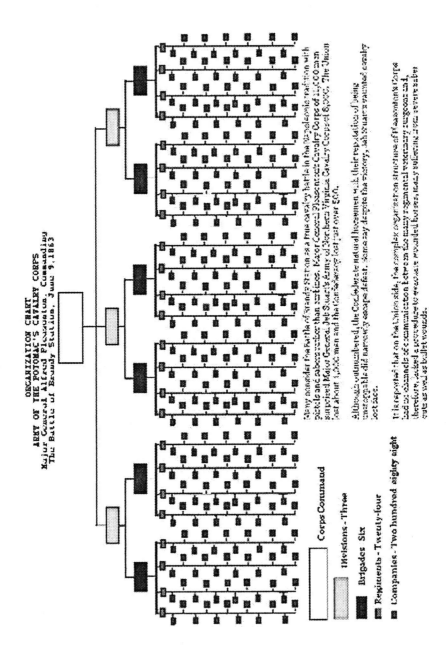

Regiment of Cavalry
Twelve Companies or Troops
Table of Organization
Act of Congress, March 3, 1863
War Department General Orders No. 110, Dated April 29, 1863

Rank	Auth. No.
Commissioned:	
Colonel	1
Lieutenant Colonel	1
Major	3
Regimental Adjutant - Lieutenant	1
Regimental Quartermaster Officer - Lieutenant	1
Regimental Commissary Officer - Lieutenant	1
Regimental Surgeon	1
Ass't. Regimental Surgeon	2
Chaplain	1
Captain	12
1st Lieutenant	12
2nd Lieutenant	12
Total Commissioned	**48**
Enlisted:	
Regimental Sergeant Major	1
Regimental Quarter Master Sgt.	1
Regimental Commissary Sgt.	1
Saddler	12
Company Quarter Master Sgt.	12
Company Commissary Sgt.	12
Veterinary Surgeon	1
Farrier/Blacksmith	24
Chief Trumpeter	1
Trumpeter	24
Wagoner	12
Hospital Steward	2
1st Sergeant	12
Sergeant	60
Corporal	96
Private – 60 minimum/78 maximum	936
Total Enlisted	**1,308**
Total Full Authorization	**1,356**

This table represents the maximum authorized strength of a regiment of cavalry as to both ranking and numbers. Rarely was a regiment manned to the maximum allowances.

With the plethora of legislative activity between July 1861 and March 1863, one would believe that the solution to the need for trained and competent veterinarians was near at hand. Conceivably this could have been true, but the capabilities provided by the Act of March 3, 1863, applied only to the six regular cavalry regiments of the Union Army.

Obviously, with the increased grade and pay the Government was reacting to the enormous increase in the need for mounts and the huge loss of animals due to wounds and disease generated by the war, thus creating the undisputed need for better-trained veterinarians.[1,4,6]

Much still remained to be done. There were hundreds of state militia and volunteer regiments of varying size and composition. The actual number of these regiments isn't clear. The Army Adjutant General reported in 1866 that there had been 232 regiments. Another source reported 272 regiments. Whatever the number, General Orders No. 110, April 29, 1863, ordered each volunteer cavalry regiment to have a veterinary surgeon, as the same as the regular cavalry regiments.[2]

Unfortunately no one has come up with a list or roster of veterinary surgeons or other veterinary personnel for even the six regular regiments.[2] Therefore, the actual total number of veterinary surgeons and farrier/blacksmiths will remain unknown.

Using the two numbers of total regiments, 232 and 272, the total possible number of veterinary surgeons and farriers/blacksmiths would compare as shown below. As provided for by the Act of March 3, 1863.

	232 Regiments	272 Regiments
(1) Veterinary Surgeons	232	272
(2) Farrier/Blacksmiths	5568	6528
Total	5800	6800

(1)   One veterinary surgeon for each regiment
(2)   Twenty-four farriers/blacksmiths for each regiment (2 per company with 12 companies in each regiment)

The significance of these figures dramatizes the enormous void between the largest possible number of veterinarians, farriers, etc., calculated on a base of unsubstantiated opinions applied to an equally unsubstantiated number of veterinary practitioners named in official records. One school of thought was that since the veterinary surgeon was not a commissioned officer, he might have been considered a civilian. Therefore, these individuals' names do not appear in the usual official military lists of regimental officers or complement rosters.[2] Where then do these names and records appear? This is yet to be discovered.

This being said, neither the Congress nor the Adjutant General had the power to force civilian veterinarians into uniform. Major General George Stoneman, Chief of Cavalry, attributed the dearth of equine doctors to the fact that there was a "deficiency of veterinary talent in the country." He offered that the problem was compounded by the "impossibility of obtaining what little talent there is for the compensation now allowed by the government." Veterinary surgeons, regardless of education or experience, were only given the non-commissioned rank of sergeant major.[3]

Considering this non-commissioned status, the veterinary surgeon, not being judged worthy of a commission, most often chose to remain in private practice, which was considerably more lucrative than military service. In addition to the disparity in pay, the few veterinarians who joined the military found no guidelines or descriptions as to what their authorities and duties were.[3,10]

One unnamed uniformed veterinarian editorialized in a popular journal of the day: "[After having created the office of veterinary surgeon], the near approach of the time for closing Congress did not permit time to define the duties of the position or the regulations by which it was to be guided, and to this day [August 1864], with the exception of an order notifying them that they are not allowed clothing or rations, the veterinary surgeons have never received any communication bearing upon the subject. In consequence, many good practitioners have never [expressed] their views of what should be done, under fear of violating some regulations with which they were unacquainted."[3]

In addition to the cavalry veterinary personnel discussed to this point, there are reports, scarce though they may be, of civilian veterinarians in the army used by the Quartermaster Department. There were probably a dozen or so veterinarians, veterinary practitioners and others who may have been hired by the Quartermaster Department seeking improvement for the care of horses and mules.[2]

There were at least five men who in one way or another were involved in veterinary activity. Two were C. M. Wood of Boston and A. S. Copeman of Utica, New York, both non-graduates of the defunct Boston Veterinary Institute. The Army of the Potomac employed them in 1861 as animal inspectors. The remaining three were: Henry Corby, a graduate of the Royal Veterinary College of London who served in the infantry and died four days after being wounded in action at Springfield, Missouri, August 10, 1861; J. C. Meyer, Sr., who graduated from the Vienna Veterinary School and, although not in the service, did reporting of some kind on a graduate veterinarian at a camp in Covington, Kentucky, in 1863; and Dr. Joseph Bushman, MRCVS of Washington, DC.[2,5]

From this group of men, President Lincoln asked Dr. Bushman to serve in the army as a veterinary sergeant. Dr. Bushman declined on the grounds that in his country (England) army veterinarians were commissioned officers.[2,3]

President Lincoln exercised his executive privilege as commander-in-chief and commissioned Dr. Bushman in the Quartermaster Corps and assigned him to the veterinary service at the Giesboro Depot. This depot, discussed later in detail, was the source of the horse and mule supply for the Army of the Potomac. In the first eight months of 1864, the cavalry of that army was remounted at least twice with approximately 40,000 horses. Dr. Bushman didn't remain long at Giesboro, stating, "I didn't last long, as a company of politicians from New York tried to foist a lot of quack medicines on the army, and I disapproved them, and soon lost my head through the machinations of the political gang."[2,3]

There is evidence that men trained in animal care were willing to offer their services. In November 1861, the senior quartermaster of the Army of the Potomac wrote to the Army Quartermaster General questioning the planned appointment of one veterinarian for duty at Cliffburne, near Washington, DC, because there were no appropriations for the monthly pay of a veterinary surgeon.[2]

Another document reveals that a John Wilson of St. Louis, Missouri, applied for the position of cavalry veterinary sergeant that had been rejected by Dr. Bushman. He claimed his qualifications for the position were having taken care of horses of the government for four months at St. Louis and Jefferson City before December 20, 1861. The trail of Mr. Wilson ends abruptly since nothing is known about the disposition of his application.[2]

Dr. John Scott of Philadelphia wrote a letter to President Lincoln on November 6, 1861. He offered a plan in which he would be appointed as "principal veterinary surgeon" to conduct six-week courses on veterinary introduction to men who might be chosen to perform such services in cavalry regiments.[2]

In December 1862, Dr. John McClure referred to the aforementioned veterinary sergeant vacancy in a letter to the army general-in-chief advising that he "declined [that position] on the grounds that no veterinary surgeon of reputation, etc. would accept a position in the army short of a Commission, etc." His real interest though was in a more important matter. Dr. McClure had a "Plan for the Prevention and Cure of the Diseases of the Horses and Mules in the Army." His plan, similar to that of Dr. John Scott in November 1861, proposed that one or more qualified surgeons should be commissioned to conduct courses of instruction in veterinary science at "horse hospitals" in Washington, DC. In a few weeks, selected grooms and stablemen could be qualified for reassignment to cavalry regiments to care for sick or injured animals.[2]

Another letter writer was Dr. John Busteed. On July 13, 1861, he wrote to the Secretary of War "to call attention to the importance of this branch of [veterinary] medical science, not only in the army, but to the agricultural interest of the country at large." He realized that qualified veterinarians would not volunteer for the army as sergeants, and suggested that the President and Secretary of War be authorized by Congress to recruit qualified veterinaries with the rank and pay of officers, and to appoint them as comparative anatomy teachers in military schools. He further recommended that there be established an army military veterinary service such as those of European armies. Dr. Busteed, in still another letter dated January 22, 1863, offered that there should be an army veterinary board to examine the qualifications of both present and future army veterinary surgeons.[2]

There isn't anything to indicate that any of these letters or other correspondence directly influenced the course of events concerning military veterinary medicine. However, the 1863 Act establishing the veterinary surgeon position was passed just months after Dr. Busteed's January 22 letter.

Despite this, some do suggest that in having their ideas and suggestions ignored, the petitioners who were civilian veterinary leaders were stimulated to organize the United States Veterinary Medical Association (USVMA) in 1863.[2,5] The name was later changed to American Veterinary Medical Association (AVMA) in 1898.[5,6,8]

Even though the Act of March 3, 1863, provided the authority to appoint veterinary surgeons, progress in recruiting such expertise was extremely slow. On October 15, 1863, more than seven months after the enactment, the Cavalry Bureau Chief reported to the Secretary of War on activities at Giesboro and other cavalry depots in part: "The number of unserviceable cavalry horses on hand…is upwards of sixteen thousand, the larger proportion of which can, with proper care and treatment, be again made fit for service in the field. One great want felt by the cavalry service is the deficiency of veterinary talent in the country, and the impossibility of obtaining what little there is for the compensation now allowed by the government."[2]

This deficiency of veterinary talent persisted. During the period 1863-1864 it was reported that 93 men applied for employment as veterinarians, but no record of their acceptance has been found.[18] A question persists. Does no record of their acceptance portend that the applicants turned down the jobs because of too little pay or did the army turn down the applicants because they lacked the necessary qualifications?

In 1863 even President Lincoln, who was reportedly sympathetic to the need and value of veterinarians, offered the rank of lieutenant to several of the "best veterinarians of the day" and was turned down because this grade offered a lower income than they could get in private practice.[17,18]

Without reference to the role of veterinary surgeons, Quartermaster General Montgomery C. Meigs stated in his 1863 annual report of his operations at remount depots that after each battle and long distance march, large numbers of "broken-down horses and mules unable to bear transportation are sent to the rear…where, at the depots they are carefully divided into classes. Those affected with glanders, or other fatal contagious diseases, are shot. Those which there is reason to believe can, in a reasonable time, by care and food, be made fit for cavalry, artillery, or ambulance service, are placed in comfortable stables, carefully tended, and fed proper and nourishing food."[2]

He further stated, "It is not too much to say that the government has already been obliged to replace many thousands of horses and mules, which, with proper understanding of, and attention to their duties on the part of the quartermasters would have been at this moment in serviceable condition… Neglect and imbecility on the part of those in charge ruin them and tax the treasury."[5,17] He concludes, "I estimate that about fifty percent of the horses which reach the depots disabled and broken-down are returned ultimately to the military service."[2]

On December 16, 1863, Dr. John Busteed, one of the founders of the USVMA and later president of the New York College of Veterinary Surgeons, wrote again to Secretary of War Edwin Stanton, "The United States Army is the only one in the civilized world without educated veterinarians."[8]

Quartermaster General Meigs criticized the Union Cavalry for the careless treatment and abuses of its horses, adding: "We have over 126 regiments of cavalry, and they have killed ten times as many horses as Rebels."[7,17]

Although never outwardly acknowledged, the veterinary service was termed a national disgrace during the Civil War. The effect of this criticism was tempered somewhat by the rationalization that the army was not entirely to blame. Considering that "war time armies, like legislative bodies, are composed of civilians temporarily serving their country, and they can be no better than the society from whence they came should be."[6]

Conceivably this "national disgrace" began as far back as General Washington's 1776 directive concerning farrier veterinarians for the artillery and continued with the hiring of partially skilled civilians, a practice that continued for well over a hundred years.[6]

Contributing most significantly to this century-plus disaster period was the attitude of the Army General Staff and most commanders who neither recognized nor admitted the need for veterinary services. Two situations exemplify the lack of regard or appreciation of veterinary services. On August 16, 1862, Colonel J. B. Fry, a Union Cavalry Chief of Staff, wrote from Huntsville Headquarters to Captain W. J. Palmer, Anderson Cavalry, Philadelphia, Pennsylvania, "Employ veterinary surgeon *cheap as possible*." The remainder of the correspondence related to raising and equipping a new regiment.[20]

In the fall of 1862, the 3rd Pennsylvania Cavalry Regiment received a number of remounts at their encampment near Dumfries, Virginia. Many of these remounts were sickly and an unidentified corporal related that Major J. C. White, in charge of the camp, selected five volunteers with a Private Eyster in charge to take care of the horses. The major directed these men to where they could find the necessary medicines and a guide book entitled, *Every Man, His Own Horse Doctor* (1738). Not one of the five knew anything about horse doctoring and apparently the guidebook was of little help. Private Eyster and his cohorts, nonetheless, prepared a concoction of flour, arsenic, other drugs, and water for which they are reported to have received compliments from the major for their good work. With this Private Eyster promptly selected two horses for treatment that night—both of which were dead by morning.[18]

Undaunted, Private Eyster repeated his dosage for the next few days until about half the newly acquired remounts were dead. This mess finally dismayed and angered Major White so that he ordered the five "horse doctors" back to their regular duty with the observation, "They are not worth shucks."[18]

Through this indifference, the army plodded along with a disorganized patchwork of animal care. Accomplishing what was done was possibly due to the fact that replacement horses were "cheap and plentiful."[6]

Secretary of War Edwin Stanton made a similar comment concerning the replacement of horses, "production of the country seems to be able to bear the immense drain upon its horses and mules, and the stock, judging from the current prices, gives no sign of exhaustion."[7] It should be mentioned that the cost of serviceable horses rose from $125 per head at the beginning of the war to $145 to $185 per head at the end of the war.[15]

As late as 1864, Secretary Stanton reported that the army acquired or used up horses at the prodigious rate of 500 animals a day.[7,11,13,14,17] During the Shenandoah Campaign, General Sheridan's force alone is reported to have required 150 new horses each day.[14,17] An amazing figure reported by some historians as fact is that the average service life for a cavalry mount was less than five months, ascribing the entire cause to poor management and lack of disease control.[6] Another source reports that the average Union trooper used about three horses a month.[13]

Figures vary significantly as to the total number of horses and mules used by both North and South during the war. In 1860, the Northern States had 4,688,678 available while the South had a little more than half that number, 2,800,000 available.[7,15] The Union had access to approximately two-thirds of the horses and mules available to both sides. Of this available number, the Union is reported to have purchased 1,031,965.[2,11] In addition to their veterinary needs, each of these animals had to be fed.

Feeding hundreds of thousands of horses every day was an enormous undertaking for both sides during the Civil War. The Union was able to

33

establish an efficient system of gathering, transporting, and storing thousands of tons of grain and hay. The sources of this forage for the North were the great horse-powered farming states of Iowa, Minnesota, and Wisconsin. Unlike other states that lost horses during the war, these states actually gained numbers for their farming operations.[7]

The forage was stored at depots, forage sheds, on wharves, and at supply bases. Between December 1862 and January 1865, the Union Quartermaster Department distributed:

- 2.7 million bushes of corn
- 20.9 million bushels of oats
- 43,311 bushels of barley
- 269,814 tons of hay
- 8,243 tons of straw[7]

Unfortunately for the South, the Confederacy wasn't able to develop the same system enjoyed by the Union or anything close to it. The transport system was so undependable that it couldn't reliably move whatever forage was available. At best, railroads were hauling barely one-sixth of the needed hay ration.[7,16] Southern farms struggled to produce forage since many farmers, and their animals, were serving with the Army. To keep up with the demand, Confederate impressment officers were scouring the Southern countryside seizing hay, grain and other crops.[7]

General Lee, his officers, and men were pleading continuously for food to sustain their horses, artillery and cavalry and others. The cavalry faced disbandment because of the search for food, and Lee's plans were often disrupted by the near starvation of his animals. In the winter of 1862-1863, he had to send his wagons 70 miles in search of forage, as if his difficulties in supplying and maneuvering his armies weren't great enough.[7,16]

Starvation of both animals and men was the scourge of the Confederacy. As to the plight of horses, at a time when the official daily ration for Union horses was 26 pounds including 12 pounds of grain,

General Lee reported to Jefferson Davis: "Some days we get a pound of corn per horse and some days more; some none. Our limit is five per day per horse."[7]

The general's dilemma of the extreme measures with which he struggled in his search for forage brought him up against an impenetrable wall called "The Supply Multiplier," so named by Fredie Steve Harris, "Horses in the Civil War," *Western Horseman*, May 1976.

The supply multiplier covered the weight of forage needed at 26 pounds per day to feed each of a given number of horses and mules times the number of days on the road. Forage transportation was based on six-mule wagons, the number of which is determined by dividing the total number of mules mustered for the march by six. This is the way it multiplied.

- 500 soldiers could be supplied by a typical six-mule wagon on a one-day round-trip from its supply base to the front.
- A 100,000-man army could be supplied by 800 wagons and 4,800 mules two days from base.
- The 16,000 cavalry and artillery horses of the above army would require an additional 800 wagons and 4,800 mules to deliver their forage.
- The 9,600 mules needed to supply the above 100,000-man army and its 16,000 cavalry and artillery horses would require an additional 400 wagons and 2,400 mules to deliver their forage.
- The 2,400 mules from immediately above needed an additional 92 wagons to carry their forage.
- The 552 mules pulling the 92 wagons from above and so forth.[7]

The product of the above multiplier to supply an army only two days from its base was as follows:

- 100,000 Men
- 16,000 Cavalry and Artillery horses
- 12,552 Mules

- 2,092 Wagons
- 673.45 metric tons of forage (hay and grain) based on 26 ounds of forage per day for each of 28,552 animals for two days.[7]

The Union operated the system effectively. The Confederacy could never master it.

Courtesy of the National Archives & Records Administration.
[Photograph 111-BA-1964]

Horse of the First Massachusetts Cavalry
Alert and Well Equipped, 1864

This is one of the hundreds of thousands of horses on the move for the U. S. Cavalry. His official daily forage ration, when available, was twenty-six pounds, of which twelve pounds were grain.

Courtesy of the National Archives & Records Administration. [Photograph 111-SC-91012]

The Army Wagon

The six-mule wagon shown in this undated photo was known as a "jerk line" freighter wagon. It was used to haul all manner of supplies including forage. It was later replaced by what was called an Escort Wagon.

At the war's beginning, the Union and Confederate remount systems were just about the same. Troopers furnished their own horses and remounts and were paid 40 or 50 cents a day. They were paid the value of the horse if it was killed in combat. Nothing was paid if the horse died of disease.[2,5,7,8,15]

The Union cavalry units were weakened by abuses. Units suffered while troopers were out hunting horses. Some men were overprotective of their favorite horses, while others escaped fighting by deliberately disabling their own horses.[7] As a deterrent to these practices, the War Department, by an order of May 1861, specified that if a trooper could not find a new horse, he would be detailed to the infantry.[15]

Throughout the war, the Union procured its animals (horses, mules, etc.) by a variety of means such as by purchase, foraging, capture or recovery of abandoned animals, and by mustering in. The latter being from states' militia and volunteer units already mounted.[2]

The acquisitions through mustering in were subject to inspection by a Union mustering officer in accordance with military regulation. He examined horses from front to rear, checking health and general condition and noted them for suitable size and age. No horse under five or over nine years old was to be accepted.[2] The officers and men of the mustering-in units were required to exhibit good horsemanship and have a practical knowledge of routine care and treatment of their mounts.[2]

Military regulations allowed for the federal mustering officer to have "some disinterested person" make the inspection, although there was no specific requirement that veterinarians would check the health and physical condition of the animals. The chances are that even if he had wanted to hire veterinarians for that purpose, there weren't enough available or willing to do the job.[2]

The Union began to profit from its errors in mid-1862. The mustering-in process was discarded, and procurement of horses and mules for the cavalry was transferred to various federal and state officials and officers. This new remount system, although a step forward, remained disorganized and scattered and hence highly susceptible to mischief.[7,15] Conspiracies developed between crooked horse contractors, horse inspectors, and military officers to sell diseased or otherwise jaded horses and mules to the army at exorbitant prices.[7]

Apparently the temptation to manipulate transactions within the horse industry was so great and so broad that a federal officer wrote that honest inspectors "were usually at their wits' ends detecting the many frauds and tricks of the horse trade...Men otherwise known to be of the staunchest integrity seem to lose all sense of the equity of things when it comes to selling or swapping horses; and this is particularly the case when the other party to the transaction is the Government, a corporate body incapable of physical suffering and devoid of sentiment."[7]

It wasn't too long before federal officials determined that more changes were needed to reduce the loss of both animals and treasury funds. Within one year, in May 1863, the Union established the Cavalry Bureau and charged it with the responsibility for the controlled purchase, care, and training of mounts for the mounted service.[7]

During the first two years of the war, the Union cavalry used up 284,000 horses. Within that same two-year period, the number of troopers was increased from five thousand to sixty thousand, which was reported to have been the maximum number of cavalrymen ever to be in the field.[1,6,7,8,17] Now, with the establishment of the Cavalry Bureau and as a consequence of the losses at the June 9, 1863, Battle of Brandy Station, the Union further began the management, care, and purchase of mounts through the reorganization of July 28, 1863. It began with specific command responsibilities.

Major General George Stoneman, Chief of the Cavalry Bureau, and Quartermaster General Montgomery Meigs reported directly to Secretary of War Edwin Stanton. Stoneman remained responsible for determining the numbers of cavalry mounts needed and their care and training. Meigs had charge of the actual purchasing of the animals, feed, supplies and building remount stations.[8] One of the first actions was to buy all of the mounts belonging to troopers already in service.[5,8]

To establish a system to collect, control and distribute horses, the reorganization order provided for the construction of six huge Cavalry Bureau Depots.[5,7,8]

These depots were established at:

- St. Louis, Missouri, and Greenville, Louisiana, for the Missouri and Gulf Departments
- Nashville, Tennessee, for the Tennessee Department
- Harrisburg, Pennsylvania, Wilmington, Delaware, and the District of Columbia (Giesboro Point) for the Department supporting the Army of the Potomac[8]

There's little doubt that the War Department planned and developed the reorganization to supply the Union army with a reliable flow of fresh and healthy horses and mules and to cut the loss of animals.[7,8]

Courtesy of the National Archives & Records Administration. [Photograph 111-B-4559]

Edwin M. Stanton
Secretary of War

Of the six Cavalry Bureau depots operated jointly by Major General Stoneman, Chief Cavalry Bureau, and Quartermaster General Meigs, Giesboro Point was by far the largest. It was said that "Nothing like Giesboro has ever existed before or since."[8]

Five thousand workers finished construction of the depot in a relatively short period of time, and it officially opened in January 1864 at a cost of $1.2 million.[8] The operating force approximated 1,500 men of various trades, three "veterinarians," many farriers, carpenters, teamsters, wheelwrights, wagon-makers and laborers.[14]

Courtesy of the Library of Congress. [Photograph LC-B814-1333]

Montgomery Meigs
Quartermaster General

Courtesy of the Library of Congress. [Photograph LC-B813-1562A]

George Stoneman
Major General
First Chief of Cavalry Bureau

Physical particulars of Giesboro Point:

Area:
- 625 acres – rental $6,000 per year

Animal facilities:
- 32 stables with 6,000 stalls
- 45 acres divided into corrals with cover for 1,000 horses each, an open space for hay racks, and water troughs
- Veterinary infirmary capable of accommodating 2,650 animals.
- Total capacity 30,000 mounts

Service structures:
- Storage buildings
- Wharves
- Grist mill
- Horse shoeing shop with 100+ blacksmiths
- Forage sheds
- Hay station

Personnel facilities:
- Barracks
- Mess houses
- Chapel

Other items:
- 210 tons of hay consumed per day*
- 180 tons of grain consumed per day*
- 700 tons of manure generated per day*

* based on full capacity of 30,000 horses

Operating costs:
- $1 million per day – at times as much as $4 million per day[8,14]

Courtesy of the National Archives & Records Administration. [Photograph 111-BA-1954]

Camp Stoneman, Giesboro Point, DC

This massive cavalry depot had stables to shelter six thousand horses. Five thousand workers built these and all of the other structures in less than nine months at a cost of $1.2 million.

Courtesy of the National Archives & Records Administration. [Photograph 111-BA-1959]

Government Horse Shoeing Shop

This 1864 photograph was taken at Giesboro Depot. The sign on the side of the building reads "Government Horse Shoeing Shop."

Estimates are that these men shod a million horses. The facility employed 100 plus blacksmiths (farriers).

Courtesy of the National Archives & Records Administration.
[Photograph 111-B-6165]

Giesboro Point, DC,
Remount Station Depot Headquarters and Stables

Based on available information, Giesboro could boast as being the only military post ever to have a graduate veterinary surgeon as a commissioned officer.[3] President Lincoln, exercising his executive privilege as commander-in-chief, had commissioned Dr. Joseph Bushman as an officer in the Quartermaster Corps in 1863. Dr. Bushman didn't last long, however, stating among other things, "I soon lost my head through the machinations of the political gang."[2,3]

Courtesy of Civil War Times Illustrated Magazine, December 1967.

Hay Depot at Giesboro Point
"Hay and straw depot at the corner
of 18ᵗʰ and F Streets, Washington DC."

Giesboro's hay station was so huge that it is reported to have "stood across" the Potomac River in Alexandria, Virginia, for fire control purposes.[8]

Within days after the Cavalry Bureau was established, Secretary of War Edwin Stanton gave Cavalry Chief General George Stoneman authority to select the Bureau's veterinary surgeons.[8] This seems to be a direct selection procedure by the Cavalry Chief—obviously a variation of the authority granted to regimental commanders by the Act of March 3, 1863, to select veterinary surgeons and submit their names for approval by the Bureau and the Secretary of War.

General Stoneman was well aware of how serious diseases, particularly glanders, had become, mainly from his experience as a cavalry commander on the Peninsula and at Fredericksburg. His intentions were to appoint experienced cavalry officers who, although not necessarily graduate veterinarians, would be more qualified than past appointments. These appointments were to serve at all of the new depots and eventually serve all regiments in the field.[8]

Interestingly enough, this authorization was no more specific as to a veterinarian's qualifications than the initial authorizing legislation. Since selection had been at the recommending officer's discretion, many were of the opinion that if a farmer, butcher, or teamster had become a sergeant, he could be a "veterinary."

At times, though, a little too much knowledge may have been disadvantageous. Dr. J. C. Meyer, Jr., a civilian graduate veterinarian, reported in 1863 that an example of this occurred at a camp in Covington, Kentucky, where a trained veterinary found that twenty-six horses had glanders and had them destroyed. He was dismissed by the regimental commander and replaced with a self-made practitioner who claimed that glanders had not been found.[5,8] It is said that it was typical of regimental officers to be more concerned with the foot conditions of horses. They sought out farriers as veterinarians to treat these conditions.[5,8,18]

Courtesy of the National Archives & Records Administration. [Photograph 111-BA-1965]

Farriers

The previous photograph was taken in August 1863 at the headquarters of the Army of the Potomac. Farriers are busy at their work. "Every company of cavalry had its own farrier enlisted as such. The men not only had to know all about the shoeing of horses, but also had to be skilled veterinary surgeons such as each regiment has at the present day, coming next in pay to a second lieutenant. Plainly visible are the small portable anvil on an overturned bucket and the business-like leather aprons of the men."[14]

Note that the descriptions of a farrier's duty as "skilled veterinary surgeons" and the pay scale differ considerably from what most research describes. Farriers' skills as veterinarians were generally described as lacking at best. The pay scale of a farrier during 1863 was listed at $15 per month, nowhere near the monthly pay of a second lieutenant, which was $75 per month.

Wanting to ensure a sound basis for his choices, General Stoneman called on Medical Inspector of the Army, Lieutenant Colonel Edward P. Vollum, to examine and report on conditions in stables and corrals at cavalry posts around Washington.[5,8] Giesboro was under construction at the time.

Colonel Vollum's findings were devastating. In his report to the Cavalry Chief he wrote, "As far as my observation extends, the treatment and management of the Government animals, in whatever condition, has been characterized by the utmost ignorance, and recklessness, and requires a most thorough overhauling."[8] Calling it the "mischief of unqualified veterinary surgeons" he mentioned one post where the veterinarian did not believe or know that glanders was contagious, so he therefore did not isolate or destroy the sick animals, exacerbating the outbreak.[5,8] At another post, 1,990 horses were diagnosed as having glanders and were destroyed. These findings confirmed the colonel's position on the disparity among animal care providers.

General Stoneman used Colonel Vollum's scathing report to support his recommendations to Secretary of War Stanton to appoint commissioned officers (captains) as inspectors and veterinary surgeons for the Cavalry Bureau.[8] Why "captains" isn't clear, and for those dubbed "veterinary surgeons," were they really "veterinarians"? It could be surmised that, at long last, those who were to practice "veterinary skills" in the Union cavalry were appointed as captains to match the rank and status of their veterinary counterparts in European armies.

Another question concerning the appointees—does the rank of captain mean "qualified" when the only law authorizing the appointment of a veterinary surgeon, the Act of March 3, 1863, set such appointments at the rank of sergeant major? Whatever the answer, the facts are that Captain John Gregsen was appointed Chief Veterinary Surgeon at Giesboro and Captain C. Baker was appointed chief inspector of horses. Both captains assumed responsibility for the horses in their charge with assistance from subordinates who may or may not have been commissioned officers.[8] Captain seemed to have become the rank of choice in that all assistant quartermasters who handled the shoeing shop, equipment, forage, transportation and personnel were also captains.[8]

With this action taken, Giesboro Point got its start and the Cavalry Bureau's odyssey got underway. No one foresaw that this new procurement system would bring with it "circumstances for the emergence of the epizootic on a grander scale than had been seen up to that time."[8]

Within a matter of just weeks after construction started, horses began to arrive at Giesboro. Corrals were probably the first structures built to handle these transients. Most were sent immediately to the front.[8]

This quick pass-through indicates that little or no inspection or processing was afforded these mounts, which is attested to by a complaint received at Bureau Headquarters from Major J. M. Gaston on October 30, 1863, stating, "On the evening of the 27th inst. two hundred and twenty-two [horses] were received in the Second Brigade of which eighty-six were unserviceable. At the same time two hundred and seventy were received in the First Brigade of which ninety-eight were unserviceable. These horses were all in poor condition, unshod and diseased, were three days on the road without any forage or any protection, the men being sent out without any ammunition...We are thus continually changing horses without deriving any benefit."[8] Recognizing that Giesboro was just getting underway, it still must be noted that this was less than an auspicious beginning.

When the Cavalry Bureau was created on May 1, 1863, Major General George Stoneman was designated the first chief. Although he had initiated procedures and established reforms to discourage fraudulent procurement practices and improve the quality of horses purchased, Stoneman could not produce significant results. He was relieved of his command on January 1, 1864, the date that Giesboro Point opened. Brigadier General Kenner Garrard, who lasted less than a month in the position, replaced him.[15]

Secretary of War Stanton then replaced Garrard with Brigadier General James H. Wilson. Wilson was said to be an aggressive young officer and did much to reduce the graft that had plagued the effort of his predecessors.[15]

He was unable, however, to locate sufficient horses for General Grant's army as it was entering the 1864 campaign. The Cavalry Bureau was having trouble remounting regular regiments, so Wilson attempted to limit the formation of new volunteer cavalry regiments. In doing this, he ran into conflict with various state governors. Foremost among these governors was Andrew Johnson, Brigadier General of Volunteers and Provisional Governor of Tennessee (and future President of the United States). It is reported that Johnson was so angered that he spared no action in his efforts to embarrass the young bureau chief.[15]

A short two months and a few days after his appointment, Wilson was relieved of his command of the Cavalry Bureau on April 7, 1864.[15] This was at his own request, but upon leaving he recommended that the command of the Bureau be turned over to Major General H. W. Halleck, the Army Chief of Staff. This was done, followed by some additional lesser appointments, since Quartermaster General Meigs saw another chance to reorganize his department.[15]

The Giesboro depot became fully operational in January 1864, and so began the initiation of a procurement system intended to ensure a "reliable source of fresh and healthy horses and mules and to reduce the loss of animals."

From January 1864 until the end of the war, approximately fifteen months, Giesboro Point processed 170,622 cavalry mounts—97,580 or 57% were distributed for service, 48,721 or 29% were sold as unfit, 24,321 or 10% died at the depot. Of these, 11,000 died within the first seven months of operation. There was mixed information on the remaining 7,174, or 4%.[5,8,14]

Post records are far from complete, which precludes an accurate description of the happenings at Giesboro. However, an early January 1864 report by Captain H. A. Dupuy mentioned that the depot was at about 73% capacity with 22,000 horses foraging daily. The same report mentioned that twenty-five laborers and a foreman had been hired to dispose of dead animals.[8]

As the year progressed they became quite busy. In September, they buried 100 animals and in the next three months, the number swelled to 1,462 burials. In December they also delivered 520 carcasses to local salvage dealers.[8]

Mortality was lower in summer months, attributable mainly to the fact that most animals were moved quickly to the front. With the corrals being less crowded during the warm months, the exposure to glanders was lessened. As the corrals filled up, the disease incidence increased.[8] As an example, the morning report for August 22 didn't show even one overnight death. However, when fall arrived, the incidence of disease increased with 331 horses being shot on just one day, November 29.[8]

For some unexplained reason, the system or procedures for selecting animals for transporting were never firmly established. Those responsible for the management of the system and procedures, such as they were, seemed to lack the discipline to make them work. On October 24, 1864, ten months after Giesboro opened, Captain C. Baker, Chief Inspector of Horses, reported the arrival at Giesboro of twenty mules from Harper's Ferry. Three of these had died en-route and eleven others had glanders.[5,8] In a letter to the officer at Harper's Ferry, he wrote in rather passive language, "I would recommend that no animals be allowed to be shipped in such a condition. This disease being contagious is almost certain to spread, assuring all other animals which are shipped in the same car. This is by no means a rare occurrence, but frequently done. I have no doubt but many animals receive this disease in this way, by shipping sound animals in cars which have been occupied by diseased ones."[8]

There's no way to determine how many animals contracted the disease at the depot and died from it at some other location. The high mortality rate would lead one to believe that almost all of the horses that had passed through Giesboro through June 1866, perhaps 250,000 altogether, were exposed to glanders.[8]

Overnight deaths from glanders reached an all-time high for a single day at 188 on January 13, 1865. The previous high of 159 had been reached just the day before. With just two months and nine days remaining in the war, the epizootic had reached its peak.[5,8]

Of the five remaining remount depots, there is only limited information on one other—the Saint Louis depot. The description of this depot and its operation does not go into the detail found for Giesboro Point. It occupied approximately 400 acres and employed a work force of 1,100 men of the same trades kept busy at Giesboro. The animal capacity was 30,000, the same as Giesboro, although only five to ten thousand horses were housed at any one time. As the horses were processed, those classed as serviceable were promptly sent out for duty. Others, classed as unserviceable, were deemed either convalescents or condemned. An estimated fifty percent of the convalescents, after "veterinary care," were returned to active duty. The condemned group was classed as "unfit for military service" and the animals were sold at public auction.[14] Approximately ¼ of the convalescent and condemned animals died or were put down.[14]

With the end of the war and the closings of Giesboro and the other depots being inevitable, the U. S. Cavalry Bureau's extraordinary undertaking came to an abrupt end. The immense depot system with all of its potential had no real chance of reaching the success level initially expected.

On this point, however, people may see the same thing in different ways. Some form their opinions on perceptions of what they envisioned a situation to have been while others have a completely different concept.

Such was the case with a photograph that appeared in *The Photographic History of the Civil War* (1911). It was a picture of a corral at Giesboro showing hundreds of horses, in several large groups, milling around as gregarious animals do. The caption written with the charm and poignancy of the times said: "Lovers of horses will appreciate, in this photograph of 1864, the characteristic friendly fashion in which the cavalry mounts are gathering in deep communion. The numerous groups of horses in the corrals of the great depot at Giesboro D.C., are apparently holding a series of conferences on their prospects in the coming battles. Presently all those who are in condition will resolve themselves into a committee of the whole and go off to war, whence they will return here only for hospital treatment. The corrals at Giesboro could easily contain a thousand horses, and they were never overcrowded. It was not until the true value of cavalry was discovered, from the experience of the first two years of warfare, that this great depot was established, but it was most efficiently handled. Giesboro was a great teacher in regard to the care of horses. Cavalrymen learned what to guard against. The knowledge was acquired partly from field service, but in great measure from the opportunity for leisurely observations, an opportunity somewhat analogous to that of a physician in a great metropolitan hospital where every kind of physical problem has to be solved."[8,14]

What the unsuspecting photographer was showing and the well-intentioned caption writer was describing was how and where glanders was spread. It was picked up at the hayracks, in the water troughs, and by the horses rubbing noses, although horse handlers commonly believed the confined spaces of stables and hospitals harbored miasma and posed the greater glanders danger.

Courtesy of the National Archives & Records Administration. [Photograph 111-B-566]

Corral, Giesboro Point, DC

Actually the separate stalls in the stables and hospitals were much safer. Glanders (an infection caused by the bacterium *Pseudomonas mallei*) spreads on contact and not through the air.[8] Unfortunately, the healthiest appearing horses, never having been sick in the hospital or convalescing in the stalls, were turned loose in the corrals where they became infected, but in most instances didn't show symptoms until they reached the army in the field.[8]

The loss of horses and mules was enormous during the Civil War. It is estimated that "between 1,200,000 and 1,500,000 horses and mules died in service."[19] There aren't any records that tally how many died in battle or died from glanders and other causes. Battles took horrendous tolls of both men and horses, but with both, the numbers that died from disease and sickness far exceeded deaths from battle wounds.[8]

The loss of soldiers is reported to be at the rate of one-third of the deaths being from battle wounds with the remaining two-thirds being caused by disease and sickness. The loss of horses is estimated to be at the rate of one tenth of the deaths being from battle wounds with the remaining nine tenths being caused by disease and sickness.[8]

John Billings, an infantryman, was reported to note, "...those who have not looked into the matter have the idea that actual combat was the chief source of the destruction of horseflesh. But, as a matter of fact, that source is probably not to be credited with one-tenth of the full losses of the army in this respect. It is to be remembered that the exigencies of the service required much of the brutes in the line of hard pulling, exposure and hunger, which conspired to use them up very rapidly; but the various diseases to which the horses are subject largely swelled the death list."[8]

Being an infantryman, it can be assumed that John Billings' observations were of horse losses among the various army services, i.e., cavalry, artillery, quartermaster, etc. thus broadening the base in support of his opinion.

As the war wound down, the military demand for horses decreased. Those horses remaining at the depots were disposed of at public sales. The public was cautioned as to the risk of buying glandered horses from the government. Farmers, both North and South, bought or secured horses to meet their agricultural needs and for other purposes. As had been warned, many of these horses carried glanders and the disease spread across the countryside.[8]

On the brighter side, the war's close brought an end to the depots where so many horses had been crowded, and so ended a significant source of the epizootic. J. R. Dodge, a statistician for the Department of Agriculture, referred to glanders as "a legacy left by the war" in his annual report for 1866. Dr John R. Page called it the "great conflagration." Call it what you will, the great epizootic was over at last.[8]

The
Confederate Side

A t the outbreak of the Civil War, the Union cavalry was small, probably less than five thousand mounted troopers. The newly formed Confederacy, of course, had to develop its entire military establishment from scratch.

To accomplish this, the Confederacy followed closely the existing guidelines of the U.S. Military. The Provisional Congress, by an enactment in March 1861, established that all mounted officers and volunteers would furnish their own mounts and associated equipment. As compensation, they would be paid forty cents per day and the value of the horse if it were killed in combat. There was no provision for value compensation if the animal died of disease.[5,7,16]

Organizationally, the cavalry of the Regular Army consisted of two regiments, with each regiment allotted ten farriers—one farrier per company. This structure also applied to volunteer regiments. In addition to the cavalry regiments, the Act provided for four light (mounted) batteries.[3]

The March 1861 Act had a more deliberate purpose than just establishing a cavalry system. In the absence of a remount system, the South granted furloughs to troopers to find replacements for the horses they lost in battle.[7,16]

One Confederate cavalryman wrote, "The theory was that the responsibility, resting upon the trooper, would ensure his proper care of the mount; but this did not work out in practice. The careful horseman, taking an interest in keeping his charge in good condition, was apt to be sometimes *too* regardful when the needs of the service demanded that he should not spare his steed, while on the other hand the temptation for a furlough—'horse details' we called them—led many to purposely neglect the proper care of the horses."[7]

This legislation would prove to be a built in fatal weakness in the South's horse supply.[7]

The Confederacy began the war with a reservoir of 2.8 million horses and mules. Unlike the Union, however, the South was not a significant horse- and mule-producing country. The North had the mid-western states such as Iowa, Minnesota, and Wisconsin to produce its animals, while the Confederacy purchased most of its horses and mules in Kentucky, Tennessee, Missouri, and Texas. These sources, more often than not, were cut off by Union forces.[7,16]

One advantage that the Confederate cavalry had over the Union cavalry was the skill of their troopers. Early on they were touted as having been born to the saddle and were admired for their natural gallantry, courage, and daring.[7] These attributes, although laudable, began to lose their luster as the horse supplies began to diminish.

The first two years revealed some interesting efforts or practices initiated to care for over-taxed and disabled animals. The Confederacy assigned their care to quartermaster officers who distributed the horses to government subsidized pasture lands where their needs were supposed to be met.[3,5,16] Untrained attendants administered what little attention these farmed- out animals received, and their contact with veterinarians was minimal. More often than not, horses were pastured on their own to recover or die. They were sometimes left without food, water, or salt. There were no veterinarians available, by contract or otherwise, to inspect or treat government stock. Diseased and healthy animals were mingled, further reducing the number of available animals.[3,5,16]

Through the remainder of the war the Confederate cavalry, unlike the Union cavalry, did not have any legislation either proposed or enacted to establish veterinary sergeant or veterinary surgeon positions.[3]

By the early months of 1863, the ravages of war were draining the South's limited horse reservoir. General Robert E. Lee stated: "Our horses and mules are in that reduced state that the labor and exposure incident to an attack will result in their destruction." He warned his chief of artillery that "The destruction of horses in the army is so great that I fear it will be impossible to supply our wants. There are not enough in the country."[5,7,16]

In desperation, the Confederacy initiated an impressment program and sent out teams to seize every possible animal and pound of forage wherever they could be found. As desperate as the South's military need for horses and mules had become, the impressment action brought desperation of equivalent intensity to farmers in their need for working animals to help them make even the most meager crop.[7]

Try as they might to reduce the public resentment that impressment had spawned, a two-edged sword had been forged. No matter which edge of the sword was sharpened, the damage resulted in an ever-deepening wound to the same cause.

General W. N. Pendleton, Confederate Chief of Artillery for the Army of Northern Virginia, wrote on this matter to Major A. H. Cole, Confederate Superintendent of Transportation, on February 18, 1864, stating "The operation of purchasing is necessarily slow because the impressments must be so conducted as to not dissatisfy the people under the smart of injustice, nor to impair the agricultural force of the country."[20]

Indifference and a complete absence of veterinarians became a cause for strong unrest among Confederate officers.[3] Obviously, with evidence of poor animal management and lack of disease control mounting, the Confederate cavalry was marching down the same road as the Union mounted service.

In August of 1863, Colonel Alexander R. Boteler, an aide to General J. E. B. Stuart, canvassed the general's brigade commanders seeking their assessments of the problems confronting the South's cavalry. One response, from Colonel John Chambliss, sharply criticized the entire cavalry operation. He emphasized the necessity for competent veterinarians and decried the South's practice of requiring troopers to provide their own mounts.[3]

"There is a crying want of veterinary surgeons to be attached to and to accompany the cavalry to provide medicines and proper treatment in the field and camp for [disabled, broken down, and exhausted] horses. The establishment of a veterinary hospital in some locality secure from cavalry raids, convenient and accessible to the main railroad communications, where cheap sheds or coverings for the winter season might be erected, where surgeons and farriers might be appointed, with the labor of hired negroes to attend the horses, would greatly enhance the efficiency of the service,... and effectually hush the discontent arising from the necessity of having to retain invalid horses in the field."[3]

Additional complaints against the Confederate cavalry system and the enormous loss of mounts on both sides at the June 9, 1863, Battle of Brandy Station, compelled the South, as did the North, to decide to reorganize its mounted service.[3,5,8,9]

In October 1863, following a recommendation of General William Nelson Pendleton, Chief of Artillery for Robert E. Lee, the Confederate War Department established a system of giant horse infirmaries.[3,8,9,16] These infirmaries, in many ways, mirrored those built by the Union during the same period.

The operational structure of this undertaking was within the Department of Field Transportation, a bureau of the Confederate Quartermaster General's Office. To head the bureau, Major A. H. Cole was designated Inspector General of Field Transportation.[3,16]

By now, the Confederacy was considering abandoning its practice of trooper ownership of cavalry mounts. All horses and mules would then be supplied by the Quartermaster Department. Heretofore, where troopers' horses, as private property, had to be cared for at the regimental level, they could now be processed as government stock.[9,16]

Opinions differ as to when or if this policy change took effect. One opinion maintains the proposed infirmaries were to be used only for the well-being of government-owned animals. Others infer that the infirmary program was intended to procure and service all horses and mules for the army.[3,8,9,16]

It's quite likely that the latter opinions were more nearly correct. Although there was no legal authority, as yet, to buy mounts for the Confederacy's troopers, there was a move afoot to scrap the old law, which had required the cavalrymen to do so. On December 29, 1864, the Confederate Congress received a bill, which they passed on February 14, 1865, and submitted to President Davis for his signature on February 23, 1865. The law required the quartermaster general to honor recommendations from field commanding generals to provide horses for dismounted troopers and to purchase the horses of any cavalry unit as needed.[3,8,9,16]

To implement the infirmary program, the Confederacy was divided into four districts. A huge infirmary was then set up within each area for the purpose of processing all unserviceable government animals.[3,4] Of the four inspection districts, the largest was at Lynchburg, Virginia. Major John G. Paxton commanded the Lynchburg Depot, which serviced General Lee's Army of Northern Virginia. It was the First District and covered the Virginia-North Carolina region.[3,8,9,16]

While the Union's horse supply seemed to be inexhaustible, the Confederacy had a much smaller horse supply at the start of the war and limited access to new fresh animals. The emphasis at their depots had to be on rehabilitation of exhausted and disabled animals rather than on simply purchasing new ones.[5]

Where some horses were available for purchase in Virginia and North Carolina, for example, the prices fixed by the Confederate impressment commissioners were far below market value. Farmers were reluctant to sell what few horses they had left at the average impressment price of $500. This price rose to $1,000 in July of 1864, while market value of fit animals varied from $1,500 to $2,500 (Confederate currency) during the same period.[16]

Some writings described the processing of horses at these depots in terms that would lead one to believe that they were operated conscientiously and efficiently. Examples of these descriptions are:

The officers in charge of the infirmaries conscientiously inspected all incoming horses and mules for evidence of disease. Those found to be infected with contagious maladies were immediately segregated for treatment while those suffering from overwork or want of provender (dry livestock food) were distributed through a network of farmers in the surrounding countryside. This program served the dual purpose of providing a healthy environment and expert care for the animals and replacing the horses and mules which were necessarily being impressed from the farmers by the government.[3]

As disabled animals entered each infirmary they were examined closely and diseased animals were segregated out. The healthy animals were then distributed to experienced caretakers in areas around the infirmary, but away from military action, where pasture was available. Diseased animals were assigned to hospitals particular to their disorder and were treated by "practiced veterinary surgeons and farriers."[5]

One claim or boast made for the Johnson County, Georgia, infirmary was that they had the remarkable accomplishment of having cured 30 cases of glanders and had healed 85% of the disabled and diseased animals that they had taken in.[5]

Some Confederate infirmary commanders, in their zeal to make their efforts appear fruitful, creatively reported these accomplishments of the Magnolia Hill Georgia infirmary to the Savannah Republican: "All the diseases to which the horse is subject are here thoroughly treated by experienced and practical veterinary surgeons and farriers, whose zeal is highly commendable and whose success has been remarkable."[3] The infirmary Commander Captain J. G. McKee of Columbus, Georgia, claimed that nearly 80% of the total number of horses received in January 1864 had been rehabilitated under the veterinary care of H. P. Davis and J. Disbrow and returned to military services.[18]

The truth is that the Confederate infirmary system, as the Union's system, began under almost insurmountable conditions. Most animals were thoroughly exhausted even before they arrived at the infirmaries. By the time they did arrive, many animals had glanders while those which were exhausted were too spent for any hope of recovery.[1,3,5,16]

As to the veterinary care that had been so glowingly reported to be provided to the overtired and diseased horses, the Confederate government did not make any verifiable provisions during the entire year of 1864 for veterinary services at any of the infirmaries.[3]

To this shortsighted, if not negligent, policy, General Pendleton, Lee's Chief of Artillery, advised the commander—"I think the very best veterinary skill in the country ought to be secured as soon as possible, to guard against a great mischief in this important interest."[3,20]

The Lynchburg, Virginia, infirmary was in existence for only fifteen months. It handled 6,875 horses: 1,057 or 15% were rehabilitated and returned to service; 2,844 or 41% died, 133 or 2% were lost or stolen, 559 or 8% were condemned and sold at public auction, and 1,483 or 22% remained on hand but were still unserviceable.[3,16]

Mules proved to be much sturdier than horses. Of the 2,885 processed at the Lynchburg infirmary, 75% or 1,644 were returned to the teamsters. The remainder lost their fight with disease or terminal exhaustion.[3,16] Whether the Confederates believed it or not, from the day the Lynchburg infirmary was opened the end of the war was a scant fifteen months away. Their efforts to salvage their cavalry needs however nobly pursued were too late to defer the inevitable.

The operation of Lynchburg was not as successful as had been hoped.[3,16] It must be remembered, however, is that it was at this place where Confederate Drs. John J. Terrell and John R. Page conducted their "landmark study" of glanders. Theirs was the first extensive clinical study of the disease in America.[8] (See Appendix A.)

In what would be the South's final effort to salvage its cavalry service, the Confederate Quartermaster's Department, in its budget estimate for the six-month period beginning January 1, 1865, included in the "incidental expenses" category, funds for the "hire of veterinary surgeons."[3]

It was the first appearance of these funds.

The first Department general order for 1865 was released on January 6 ordering, in part, the following:

> VII. To prevent the loss from disease of animals in the service, cavalry and other private animals will be included by inspectors of field transportation in their inspections. They will dispose of those affected with contagious diseases, as prescribed by...Army Regulations. Those otherwise unfit for present service will be mustered out by the inspectors or, as they may elect, sent from the field, to be recruited with the public animals.[3]

Retrospective

In April 1861, the United States was nearing the end of its 85th year as a sovereign nation. These eighty-five years were not without struggle and growing pains. There were forty-two years of conflicts during this time, varying in intensity from the Northwest Indian Wars to the Mexican-American War. The new republic had to recover from a period of economic hardships caused by the loss of export markets, monetary collapse, depression and state bankruptcies.[14,21] Eighty percent of America's population was rural and the economy was heavily agricultural. The rural population was the primary source of the national income. Despite this demographic, colleges of the day had little, if any, interest in providing instruction in agriculture or farming in general including veterinary care. Instead they followed the English Universities' concentration on the classics, i.e., religion, medicine, and the law.[22]

With the onset of the Civil War, this indifference toward educating the common population would prove costly. The military demand for horses and mules increased dramatically, and the situation thus created was an absolute enigma. The Union had the wherewithal to construct six huge infirmaries and remount depots. These facilities, built in record time, were designed and equipped to procure, provide care, and distribute the hundreds of thousands of horses and mules that the wartime military would require. There had never before been anything built to equal them.[8] The potential for these infirmaries could have been unlimited, but for the fact that the Union lacked the wherewithal to staff them with an experienced and efficient veterinary service.

Apparently both the lack of time and resistance to more formal training for farriers were deterrents to producing an adequate number of more highly skilled veterinary practitioners.[18] It seems though that farriers, long the military's choice as horse doctors, practiced their trade at the depots and among the military units in the field. Many believe that this "lack of an efficient veterinary service" was responsible, in part, for the loss of over a million animals that "died in service."[18] The Confederacy fared no better in its efforts to sustain its animal resource. This grim assessment isn't to say that there wasn't anything being done to advance the veterinary profession.

On July 2, 1862, President Lincoln signed the Morrill Act into law. Known as the Land-Grant Act, the law was first introduced in 1857 but was blocked by the South and vetoed by President Buchanan.[22,23]

Once enacted, states that accepted the Act were granted federal land, which they were to sell and convert the proceeds into the establishment of colleges in mechanical arts, agriculture and military tactics.[22,23,24] Iowa, Vermont, and Connecticut accepted the Act in 1862, and by the end of 1863 another fourteen states adopted the law. The significance of the Land-Grant Act cannot be overstated. Several of the newly established colleges introduced veterinary subjects, then studies in veterinary science, and at last schools of veterinary medicine.[22,23,24]

On June 9, 1863, as the most furious cavalry battle in American history raged at Brandy Station, Virginia, six veterinarians met in New York and formed the United States Veterinary Medical Association (USVMA) known today as the American Veterinary Medical Association (AVMA). The zeal of these forward-looking men is credited with stimulating significantly the advancement of the nation's veterinary profession.[2,5,6,8]

Within about fifteen months after the war's end, Congress, by the Act of July 28, 1866, authorized four additional cavalry regiments. The implementing orders authorized two veterinary surgeons for each of the four new regiments. Of the eight additional veterinary surgeons authorized, four were paid $100 each per month. The other four were each paid $75 per month. The act didn't affect the six cavalry regiments reorganized on March 3, 1863, but the authorization for eight new positions with a pay increase for four of them was a substantial stride forward to meeting the military's veterinary needs.[17]

Despite continued resistance toward veterinary service by some general officers, progress, although slow, was deliberate. War Deptartment General Orders No. 36, March 27, 1879, required that army veterinary applicants "shall be graduates of recognized veterinary colleges." The era of non-professionals and sometimes quackery in veterinary service was nearing its end.[17]

Although much remained to be done, there's little doubt that direct and positive efforts were underway to advance the art of veterinary care and avoid a recurrence of the enormous waste of animal life experienced during the Civil War. The Army's long-awaited new era of competent professional animal care got under way in 1916 with the establishment of the Army Veterinary Corps with veterinarians as commissioned officers.

Endnotes

[1] Robert H. Dunlop, Cert. Agr., D.V.M., Ph.D., FAAVPT, MRCVS, MACVSc., LL.D.(Hon) and Williams, David J., MS, FAMI, MMAA. "Care of Animals Used in Transport, War, and Sport," *Veterinary Medicine – an Illustrated History*, pp. 474-76.

[2] Miller, Everett B. VMD. *A Veterinarian's Notes on the Civil War*, July 22, 1980.

[3] Nick Nichols. "Too Little Too Late," *War Horse – The Equine and the Civil War*, 1988, Chapter 6.

[4] Miller, Everett B. LtC, Veterinary Corps, United States Army. "Military Veterinary Medicine," *The American Veterinary Profession, its Background and Development*, Chapter 19.

[5] Quigley, Michelle. "Veterinary Medicine in the American Civil War," *Veterinary Heritage*, Volume 24, No. 2. November 2001, pp. 33-37.

[6] Kester, Wayne O. DVM. "Development of Equine Veterinary Medicine in the United States," *Journal of the American Veterinary Medical Association*, Volume 169, No. 1. pp. 50-51.

[7] Harris, Fredie Steve. "Horses in the Civil War," *Western Horseman*, May 1976, pp. 66-68.

[8] Sharrer, G. Terry, Curator of Agriculture, Smithsonian Institution, National Museum of American History, Washington, D.C. "The Great Glanders Epizootic, 1861-1866, A Civil War Legacy," *Agricultural History*, Vol. 69 No. 1, Winter 1995, pp. 79-97.

[9] "The Confederate Cavalry and the Great Glanders Epizootic," *the Civil War Quartermaster's Glanders Stable*, Lynchburg, Virginia.

[10] Hautz, August V., Captain Sixth U.S. Cavalry, Brigadier General U.S. Volunteers. *The 1865 Customs of Service for Non-commissioned Officers and Soldiers*, 1865, Second Edition. Pages 69-71, Paragraphs 208-212, Page 286.

[11] "Phase One, Rush to Colors, Warriors and Patriots," An *Illustrated History of the Civil War*, pages 48-49.

[12] Katcher, Philip. "The Battle of Brandy Station," *Battle History of the Civil War*, Pages 78-79.

[13] Lewis, Bill. "Horses and Mules: Gap in Civil War Research," *Civil War Times Illustrated*, May 1959.

[14] Miller, Francis Trevelyan. *Photographic History of the Civil War*. Volume 4, 1911, pages 38, 45, 65, 68, 320, 322, 325, 328.

[15] Barton, John V. "The Procurement of Horses," *Civil War Times Illustrated*, Dec. 1967, pp. 17-24.

[16] Ramsdell, Charles. "General Robert E. Lee's Horse Supply," *American Historical Review*, Volume 25, Issue 4, 1930 pp. 758-777.

[17] Merillat, Louis A., Lt. Col., Vet. Res. and Campbell, Delwin M. Lt. Col., Vet. Res., *Veterinary Military History of the United States*, Volume 1, Pages 80, 86, 87, 117, 151, 153-155, 159-160, 162, 170.

[18] Stewart, Miller J. "Too Little, Too Late, The Veterinary Services of the Civil War," *Veterinary History*, Nov. 1983, Pages 894-898.

[19] Howard, Robert West. "The Conquerors," *The Horse in America*, 1965, Page 191.

[20] *The War of the Rebellion; A Compilation of the Official Records of the Union and Confederate Armies*, Series III-Volume IV. Ser. 1 Vol. 16 Pages 348-349; Ser. 1 Vol. 33, Pages 1182-1183, 1188-1189; Ser. 3 Vol. 1 Page 681; Ser. 3 Vol. 2 Pages 786-788; Ser. 3 Vol. 3 Pages 1119-1120; Ser. 3 Vol. 4 Pages 285-286; Ser. 3 Vol. 5 Pages 251-252.

[21] Marley, David F. *Wars of the Americas, A Chronology of Armed Conflict in the New World*, 1492 to the Present, pp 348, 442, 464, 500.

[22] Place, Nick T., Assistant Professor. "Events Leading to the Establishment of Land-Grant Universities," *IFAS/University of Florida, Land and Sea Grant,* www.ifsas.ufl.edu/is_grant/whatislg.htm.

[23] "Backgrounder on the Morrill Act," *U.S. Statutes at Large 12* (1862): 503, usinfo.state.gov/usa/infousa/facts/democrac/27.htm.

[24] "Centennial Fact Book – 1862-1962,"*Amer. Association of Land Grant Colleges and State Universities*, p. 31.

Appendix A

———◆·◆·◆———

GLANDERS

Was it "A legacy left by the war" or the "Great Conflagration"?

Glanders* reaches back into antiquity. It is a highly contagious disease that affects horses, mules, humans, and house cats. Both Hippocrates (460-360BC) and Aristotle (384-342BC) worked with the disease. *Pseudomonas mallei*, a bacterium, was identified as the causative agent of this disease.

A cure for the disease has never been developed, but it was eradicated from the United States in 1934. Quarantine has kept it from the country since then.[n]

Being an ancient disease, glanders is deep in military history. It can be traced back to Constantine the Great's reign (AD 324-37). Glanders plagued the Crusaders and during the Seven Years War (1756-63), glanders was so severe that Louis XV (1714-74) established the Ecole Nationale Veterinaire at Lyons to examine the effect of the disease on the French cavalry.[8]

Glanders was possibly introduced to America by the British cavalry during the Revolution. It wasn't until the Second Seminole War

(1835-42) that it first became noticed as a problem.[8] It became more firmly established as the American horse population increased, spurred on by the importation of horses of varying types and breeds from Britain during the 1850s. The Civil War followed, with the armies of both North and South creating vast concentrations of horses and mules susceptible to glanders. Thus the epizootic* began.[8]

Glanders (a zoonosis*) is a lethal and highly contagious febrile* disease of horses, donkeys, and mules. It can, at times, be transmitted to other animals and humans. The disease attacks the mucous membranes and lymphatic systems in animals. In acute* cases, glanders is characterized by ulceration of the nose, involving the cartilage and bone.

Infected animals developed high fevers and a thick, sticky nasal discharge called, interestingly enough, "snot" from the Dutch, "snott" from the Norwegian, and "gasnott" from the old English.[9] As the disease advanced, the liver, spleen, and respiratory system became involved. The lymph nodes swelled into what are known as farcy buds*. Death usually followed within a few days after these symptoms appeared.[5,8]

Chronic* glanders assumed three forms: nasal, pulmonary, and cutaneous*. It was possible for affected animals to experience all three forms at the same time. Animals, so infected, might spread the disease for years and yet be only slightly weakened themselves. There were no assurances of immunity for horses that had recovered from glanders. Although many treatments were tried, there was no prophylaxis* or effective medicines in existence.[8]

Two Confederate army surgeons stationed at Lynchburg, Virginia, performed the first clinical study of glanders in America. Drs. John J. Terrell and John R. Page, graduates of Jefferson Medical College in Philadelphia, and the University of Virginia, respectively, were designated by Confederate Quartermaster, Major James G. Paxton, to research the "baneful scourge" of glanders ravaging horses, mules and humans alike.[5,8,9]

The study involved nineteen horses, seven of which were monitored and examined during the full progression of the disease through the final stages and ultimate death. The remaining twelve horses were "put down" and Drs. Page and Terrell performed necropsies* on them. The landmark examination pursued the disease throughout the animals' systems revealing, as stated by Dr. Page, "the whole venous* and lymphatic* system of vessels were diseased." The evidence being "cheesy pus" wherever they made a cut. They also reproduced the "pathological* character" by inoculating several healthy horses with the virus. Dr. Page and Dr. Terrell concluded, "The direct exciting cause was contagion*, the direct transmission of disease, by means of a specific virus*, from one animal to another, by artificial or natural inoculation...."[5,8]

They contrasted "contagion" as being caused by direct contact, as stated above, with "infections"* being carried by contaminants* of the air, water, or food.[5,8]

By identifying "contagion" as a direct contact cause, the study findings contradicted the ancient Greek humoral* theory that "infections" resulted from contaminants that produced the morbid* states. The humoral* theory supposed that health, both human and animal, was harbored in a balance of four essential fluids—blood, yellow bile*, black bile, and phlegm*. From the earliest times, doctors knew that when an animal had a constant temperature, the humors were in balance and the animal was healthy. When contaminants from the surroundings caused body temperatures to rise above normal and throw the humors out of balance, diseases would occur. Treatment consisted of purging, bleeding, medicines, and nutritious food with the hope of bringing the humors back into balance.[5,8]

The humoral theory was believed to have explained so many diseases and morbid conditions that it "remained the central concept of biomedical thought, and even western philosophy, from 400 BC until the 1860's."[8]

The Page and Terrell research, as extensive as it was, did not produce a cure for glanders. They determined that prevention was the only means by which it could be controlled and kept from spreading.

Keep in mind that horses and mules are gregarious animals. They congregate in groups and use their noses not only to smell but to identify and communicate with each other. It was very important then, where practicable, to control the congregating, to avoid the use of communal watering troughs, and to house the animals in uncrowded, well-ventilated, sanitary stable facilities.[8,9]

The horses' noses, so important to their enjoyment of their natural mode of living, could well serve as the conduit to carry the cause of severe suffering and death—glanders.

---

*See glossary.

Glanders Glossary

ACUTE – A term used to describe a disorder or symptom that comes on suddenly.

BILE – Yellow or greenish liquid secreted by the liver.

CHRONIC – Describes a disorder or set of symptoms that has persisted for a period of time.

CONTAGION – Direct transmission of a disease from one animal to another.

CUTANEOUS – Pertaining to the skin.

EPIZOOTIC – Of diseases spread rapidly among animals.

FARCY BUDS – An ulcerated swelling.

FEBRILE – Pertaining to or marked by fever.

GLANDERS – A highly contagious disease of horses, mules and sometimes other animals and humans. Attacks the mucous membranes and lymphatic system (zoonosis).

HUMORAL THEORY – Ancient Greek theory that health was in the balance of four fluids (humors) – blood, yellow bile, black bile, and phlegm.

INFECTIONS – Carried by contaminants of the air, water, or food.

LYMPHATIC – Pertaining to, containing or conveying lymph, i.e. a yellowish coaguable fluid containing white blood cells.

MORBID – The state or condition of being diseased.

NECROPSIES - A medical term for an autopsy (postmortem examination) of animals.

PATHOLOGICAL – Relating to disease or to pathology (the study of disease).

PHLEGM – The thick mucus secreted in the respiratory passages and discharged through the mouth.

PROPHYLAXIS – A drug, procedure, or piece of equipment used to prevent disease.

PSEUDOMONAS MALLEI – The disease organism of glanders.

PURGING – To rid of whatever is impure or undesirable – to remove by cleansing or purifying.

VENOUS – Of, pertaining to or of the nature of a vein or veins.

VIRUS – (In this writing poison, any poison). Smallest known type of infectious agent.

ZOONOSIS – Any infectious or parasitic disease of animals that can be transmitted to humans.

Montage of the Greek ~ Humoral Theory

Vital Fluids	Element of Creation	Qualities of the Seasons	Basic Temperaments
Blood	Air	Spring (Moist)	Sanguine
Yellow Bile	Fire	Summer (Hot)	Irritable
Black Bile	Earth	Fall (Dry)	Melancholy
Phlegm	Water	Winter (Cold)	Phlegmatic

The vital fluids (humors) represented the four "elements" of creation reflecting the qualities of the four seasons and their four basic temperaments.[8]

Appendix B

Diseases and Illnesses of Horses

Colic: A dangerous ailment caused by constipation and resultant gas pressures against the heart. Can be fatal.

Distemper: [Strangles] An infectious, transmissible disease characterized by inflammation of the upper respiratory tract and most often by abessation of the adjacent lymph nodes.

Equine Encephalomyelitis: Inflammation of the brain and spinal cord.

Equine Infectious Anemia: [Swamp fever] An acute or chronic viral disease, found wherever there are horses. The virus is related to the human immunodeficiency virus but is not known to infect man.

Equine Influenza: An acute highly contagious febrile respiratory disease.

Farcy: A form of the disease glanders, chiefly affecting the superficial lymphatics and the skin of horses.

Grease Heels: A disease of the heels and legs of horses characterized by a white offensive greasy discharge from the heels of the horse.

Heaves: A lung disease caused by the dilation of air cells in a lung.

Laminitis: A painful inflammation in the wall of a hoof.

Pleuropneumonia: An acute or chronic inflammation of the pleural membranes presumably originating in the lung(s), and characterized by signs related to pleural pain and pleural effusion.

Potomac Horse Fever: An acute diarrheal syndrome that was first described in horses in close proximity to the Potomac River.

Ringbone: An abnormal bony growth just above the hoof on the pastern. Can be caused by travel over hard surfaces.

Spavin: A disease of the hocks. Manifested in two forms, bone – abnormal enlargement of the inner or lower part of the joint, bog – an enlargement of the joint tissue.

Splint: A bony growth on the inside of the foreleg. Caused usually by travel on hard surfaces.

Thrush: An inflammation in the cleft of the hoof's frog causing softening of the horn and a foul-smelling discharge.

Vesicular Stomatitis: Characterized by fever and vesicles on the mucous membranes of the mouth, epithelium of the tongue, teats, soles of the feet, coronary band, and occasionally other parts of the body.

Sources

Howard, Robert West, *The Horse in America*.

Sharrer, G. Terry, *Livestock and the Disease Crisis of the Civil War*.

The Merck Veterinary Manual.

IN MEMORIAM
The Civil War Horse
Neglected in Life – Respected in Death

They strained with their loads until they dropped. They carried their troopers until they could advance no farther. They were rewarded with neglect, indifference and carelessness. They died. Salvagers then bid for their bones and promised "to satisfy all parties for damages."

To this ignominious request someone, at last, said ENOUGH!

Quartermaster General's Office
Washington DC 19th Oct. 1865.

Mr. Jacob Groat,
Washington DC
Sir:

The letter of Maj. Gen. Ingalls of the 25th September last, to Major Gen. Augur, stating that you desire a permit to dig up dead animals in Virginia, has been received.

The Quartermaster General will not give his consent or authorization to dig up the dead animals of the army. Having died in service he thinks they ought to rest in peace.

The owners of the land in which they are buried should not be disturbed.

Very respectfully,
Your Obdt Servt,
(Signed) M.C. Meigs
Brt. Maj. Genl.
Qr. Mr. Genl.

Courtesy of the National Archives & Records Administration

Printed in the United States
33458LVS00003B/165

9 781413 773262